THE TEXT BOOK

OF

CRYPTIC MASONRY.

A MANUAL OF INSTRUCTIONS

IN THE DEGREES OF

ROYAL MASTER, SELECT MASTER AND SUPER-EXCELLENT MASTER.

TOGETHER WITH THE CEREMONIES OF

INSTALLING THE OFFICERS, CONSTITUTING AND DEDICATING A COUNCIL,

AND

INSTALLING THE OFFICERS OF A GRAND COUNCIL.

BY

JACKSON H. CHASE, 33°,

GRAND LECTURER TO GRAND COUNCIL OF ROYAL AND SELECT MASTERS OF THE STATE OF NEW YORK.

NEW YORK:
MASONIC PUBLISHING COMPANY,
432 BROOME STREET.
1870.

The Textbook of Cryptic Masonry

A Cornerstone Book
Published by Cornerstone Book Publishers
Copyright © 2008 by Cornerstone Book Publishers

All rights reserved under International and Pan-American Copyright Conventions. No part of this book may be reproduced in any manner without permission in writing from the copyright holder, except by a reviewer, who may quote brief passages in a review.

Cornerstone Book Publishers
New Orleans, LA

First Cornerstone Edition - 2008

www.cornerstonepublishers.com

ISBN: 1-934935-26-3
ISBN 13: 978-1-934935-26-2

MADE IN THE USA

PREFACE.

The present work has been compiled as a "Text Book" for Officers and Companions of Councils of Royal and Select Masters.

That such a Manual has long been needed, will be acknowledged by all conversant with Cryptic Masonry.

The manuscript was submitted to our late M. P. Rev. Charles H. Platt, G. M., for his examination, and received his unqualified approval.

It has been arranged in strict conformity to the work as approved by him, and adopted by the Grand Council of Royal and Select Masters of the State of New York, and is respectfully submitted to the fraternal consideration of Cryptic Companions, wheresoever dispersed.

JACKSON H. CHASE, 33°

ALBANY, N. Y., *Dec.*, 1869.

CONTENTS.

ROYAL MASTER.....	7
Opening...	9
History...	15
SELECT MASTER,.....	19
Prayer at Opening..	21
Reception....	22
History...	23
Charge to the Candidate.....	34
SUPER-EXCELLENT MASTER...	37
Reception....	39
Hymn...	45
History..	50
INSTALLATION OF THE OFFICERS OF A SUBORDINATE COUNCIL...	55
CONSTITUTING AND DEDICATING COUNCILS....	71
INSTALLATION OF THE OFFICERS OF THE GRAND COUNCIL......	77

ROYAL MASTER.

HIS degree is conferred on Royal Arch Masons only, and is preparatory to the Select Master's degree.

The ceremonies are impressive as well as replete with useful and valuable information. It is intimately connected with and explains many mysteries of the Royal Arch.

A Council of Royal Masters is composed of the following officers:

1. THRICE ILLUSTRIOUS MASTER, representing King Solomon;
2. RIGHT ILLUSTRIOUS DEPUTY MASTER, representing Hiram, King of Tyre;
3. ILLUSTRIOUS PRINCIPAL CONDUCTOR OF THE WORKS, representing Hiram Abif;
4. MASTER OF THE EXCHEQUER or TREASURER;
5. RECORDER;
6. CAPTAIN OF THE GUARDS;
7. CONDUCTOR OF THE COUNCIL;
8. STEWARD;
9. SENTINEL;

The following diagram will show the stations of the officers:

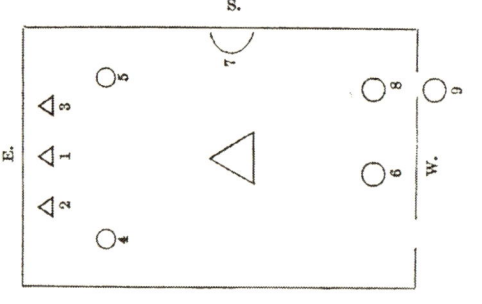

OPENING.

Now and ever may our Supreme Benefactor preside in all our Councils. May He direct us to such measures as He himself shall approve and be pleased to bless. May we ever be favored of God. May our Sanctuary be the pride of the worthy, the resort and seat of the moral virtues, the asylum of the oppressed, a name and a praise in the whole earth until the last of time shall bury the empires of the world in undistinguished ruin. Amen. So mote it be.

SECTION I.

* * * * * *

And Solomon made all the vessels that pertained unto the house of the Lord: the altar of gold and the table of gold, whereupon the shew-bread was; and the candlesticks of pure gold; five on the right side, and five on the left, before the oracle; with the flowers and the lamps, and the tongs of gold; and the bowls, and the snuffers, and the basins, and the spoons, and the censers of pure gold; and the hinges of gold, both for the doors of the inner house, the most holy place, and for the doors of the house, to wit, of the Temple. So Hiram made an end of doing all the work that he had made King Solomon for the house of the Lord.— 1 KING. vii. 48–50 & 40.

* * * * * *

"Remove far from me vanity and lies; give me neither poverty nor riches; feed me with food convenient for me; lest I be full, and deny thee and say, Who is the Lord? or lest I be poor and steal, and take the name of my God in vain."

* * * * * *

Companion Adoniram, death is a subject that admits of no levity when mentioned by mortal man. The *young may* die, the *old must* die, the wisest knoweth not how soon. The youngest E∴ A∴ upon the checkered pavement below, dwells even in the shadow of death, while the invisible hand extends equally above K∴ S∴ on his ivory throne. We walk upon the ashes of the generations who have gone this way before us, and our bodies must soon crumble into dust. It is not for me, Companion Adoniram, to hope that I shall escape from the common doom of man, but when * * * * * * Death terminates the labor of a man. There is no work, nor device, nor knowledge, nor wisdom in the grave. The most gifted of mortal kings thus meditates: "Brief life is here our portion." Speedily do we hasten to the end of these cares and labors. What an incentive is, this to an industrious use of our faculties, that we should labor diligently to complete that inner temple for God's eternal praise, and be ready to sleep in peace, as the night cometh when no man can work. My work, Companion Adoniram, is not finished, though I have labored faithfully and long, but when * * * * * * *. Companion Adoniram, it is through the gate of death that we find an entrance to the place of wages, refreshment and rest. The Supreme Master of the Universe before whom we bow in adoration, and whose All-seeing Eye has marked our labors in the Lodge below, promises to spread before us in the stupendous Lodge above all the joys and glories of His Eternal Sabbath. After the strong hand of death has leveled all in the humiliation of the grave, the Almighty hand of the Supreme Master shall prevail and exalt every brother to the glorious companionship of that undissolving Lodge. There the designs upon the Trestle-board will be seen completed. There the adoration of the twelfth hour will be the everlasting joy. There the noon-tide of bliss will eternally shine. There the scales of doubt and darkness shall fall from my eyes, and the wise purposes of the Divine Architect be displayed in all their splendor. With this light of faith beaming upon me "O Death where is thy sting?" My hope, Companion Adoniram, rests in the higher Lodge to which I am advancing, and when * * * * * * *.

SECTION II.

* * * * * *

And he set the cherubims within the inner house; and they stretched forth the wings of the cherubims, so that the wing of the one touched the one wall; and the wing of the other cherub touched the other wall; and their wings touched one another in the midst of the house.—1 Kings vi. 27.

And Solomon made all the vessels that pertained unto the house of the Lord: the altar of gold and the table of gold, whereupon the shew-bread was; and the candlesticks of pure gold; five on the right side, and five on the left, before the oracle; with the flowers and the lamps, and the tongs of gold; and the bowls and the snuffers, and the basins, and the spoons, and the censers of pure gold; and the hinges of gold, both for the doors of the inner house, the most holy place, and for the doors of the house, to wit, of the Temple. So Hiram made an end of doing all the work that he had made King Solomon for the house of the Lord.— I Kings. vii. 48–50· & 40.

* * * * * *

And behold I come quickly; and my reward is with me, to give every man according as his work shall be. I am Alpha

ROYAL MASTER. 15

and Omega, the beginning and the end, the first and the last. Blessed are they that do his commandments, that they may have a right to the tree of life, and may enter in through the gates into the city.—Rev. xxii. 12–14.

HISTORY.

This degree originated in consequence of a conversation between our Grand Master, H∴ A∴, and Adoniram, just before the death of the former.

Adoniram was one of the * * *. He was also one of the * * *.

After the S∴ S∴ was completed and a portion of the furniture deposited therein, Adoniram * * *. At high twelve, when the craft were called from labor to refreshment, * * *. After the rest of the craftsmen had retired, Adoniram * * *.

* This conversation having been related to K∴ S∴ by Adoniram * * * to which this is preparatory.

The furniture of the S∴ S∴ consisted of many holy vessels made of pure gold, but the most important there, was the Ark of the Covenant, called the glory of Israel, which was seated in the middle of the holy place, under the wings of the cherubim. It was a small chest or coffer, three feet nine inches long and two feet three inches wide and deep. It was made of wood, excepting only the mercy seat, but overlaid with gold both inside and out. It had a ledge of gold surrounding it at the top, into which the cover, called the mercy-seat, was let in. The mercy-seat was of solid gold, the thickness of an hands breadth; at the two ends were two cherubim, looking inward toward each other, with their wings expanded; which, embracing the whole circumference of the mercy seat, they met on each side, in the middle; all of the Rabbins say it was made out of the same mass, without any soldering of parts.

Here the *Shekinah*, or Divine Presence, rested, and was visible in the appearance of a cloud over it. From hence the Bathkoll issued, and gave answers when God was consulted. And hence it is, that God is said in the Scripture, to dwell between the cherubim; that is between the cherubim on the mercy-seat, because there was the seat or throne of the visible appearance of his glory among them.

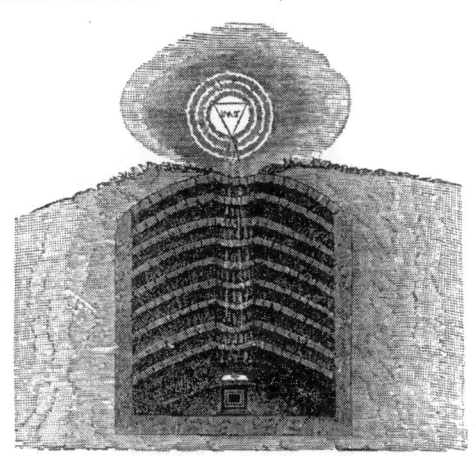

SELECT MASTER.

HIS degree is the summit and perfection of ancient Masonry; and without which the history of the Royal Arch Degree can hardly be said to be complete. It rationally accounts for the concealment and preservation of those essentials of the craft, which were brought to light at the erection of the second temple; and which lay concealed from the Masonic eye for four hundred and seventy years. Many particulars relative to those few who were selected, for their superior skill, to complete an important part of King Solomon's temple, are explained. And here, too, is exemplified an instance of *justice* and *mrcy* by our ancient patron, toward one of the craft who was led to disobey his commands by an *over-zealous* attachment for the Institution. It ends with a description of a particular circumstance, which characterizes the degree.

A Council of Select Masters is composed of the following officers:

1. THRICE ILLUSTRIOUS MASTER, as K∴ S∴.
2. RIGHT ILLUSTRIOUS DEPUTY MASTER, as H∴ K∴ of T∴.
3. ILLUSTRIOUS PRINCIPAL CONDUCTOR OF THE WORKS, as H∴ A∴.
4. TREASURER.
5. RECORDER.
6. CAPTAIN OF THE GUARDS, as A∴.
7. CONDUCTOR OF THE COUNCIL, as A∴.
8. STEWARD.
9. SENTINEL.

STATIONS.

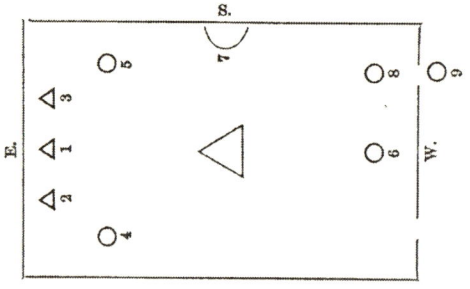

SELECT MASTER. 21

PRAYER AT OPENING A COUNCIL.

May the Supreme Grand Master graciously preside over all our counsels, and direct us in all such things as he will be pleased to approve and bless. May our profession as Masons be the rule of our conduct as men. May our secret retreat ever continue to be the resort of the *just* and *merciful;* the seat of the moral virtues, and the home of the *select.* So mote it be.

The following Psalm is read:

His foundation is in the holy mountains. The Lord loveth the gates of Zion more than all the dwellings of Jacob. Glorious things are spoken of thee, O city of God. Selah. I will make mention of Rahab and Babylon to them that know me. Behold, Philistia, and Tyre, with Ethiopia: this man was born there. And of Zion it shall be said, This and that man was born in her: and the Highest himself shall establish her. The Lord shall count, when he writeth up the people, that this man was born there. Selah.

As well the singers, as the players on instruments, shall be there: all my springs are in thee.—Psalm lxxxvii.

RECEPTION.

The following passages of Scripture are introduced and explained:

And it came to pass, when Moses had made an end of writing the words of this law in a book, until they were finished, that Moses commanded the Levites, which bore the Ark of the Covenant of the Lord, saying, Take this Book of the Law, and put it in the side of Ark of the Covenant of the Lord your God, that it may be there for a witness against thee.—Deut. xxxi. 24-26.

* * * * * *

And Moses said, This is the thing which the Lord commandeth, Fill an omer of it to be kept for your generations; that they may see the bread wherewith I have fed you in the wilderness, when I brought you forth from the land of Egypt. And Moses said unto Aaron, Take a Pot, and put an omer

SELECT MASTER. 23

full of Manna therein, and lay it up before the Lord, to be kept for your generations. As the Lord commanded Moses, so Aaron laid it up before the testimony to be kept.—Exod. 32-34,

* * * * * *

And the Lord said unto Moses, Bring Aaron's Rod again before the testimony, to be kept for a token.—Numb. xvii. 10.

* * * * * *

HISTORY:

In giving the history of this degree we revert to the building of the temple. Our three Grand Masters, Solomon King of Israel, Hiram King of Tyre and Hiram Abif being in possession of the writings of Moses and the prophets, well knew that if the children of Israel deviated from the laws therein contained, their enemies would be let loose upon them, their cities and temples sacked, ruined and destroyed, and all the sacred treasures in the S∴ S∴ would be forever lost.

In order to prevent this evil * * *. This secret vault * * *, place to deposit a true copy of all the holy vessels and sacred treasures contained * * * Grand Council to confer * * *. There were employed to work on the other eight arches, twenty-two men from Gebal, a city in Phœnicia, together with Ahishar and Adoniram, all of whom were well skilled in the arts and sciences generally, but particularly in sculpture. Their hours of labor were * * *. During the erection of this vault a circumstance occurred which characterizes this degree and upon which the ceremony of initiation is founded. * * * and for a long time he grieved in silence. * * *, meaning when the temple was completed and he should * * *. This satisfied him. * * *. When the ninth arch was completed * * * Ark of the Covenant and placed within * * * copy of the Book of the Law, and that it might be known by whom and for what purpose it was deposited, * * * When the deposit was made * * *, yet on their return if found, by means of the other two languages it might be restored, and that it might be known and distinguished * * *, by which means was preserved and brought * * *. It was then lost. * * *. It was again restored to the craft, in whose possession we trust it will forever remain.

The Lecture may end here with the charge or be continued as follows:

There may be an inquiry in your mind what was the nature of the word that rendered the Jews so anxious to keep possession; how came it in their possession, and of what importance was it to them—this part Solomon has allusion to when the Master's word was lost.

Zeroaster (who flourished about 800 years before the building of the temple) in the Zendavista writes, "There are names given by God himself to every nation, of unspeakable efficacy in the mysteries." Therefore, this word in the minds of the Jews was of unspeakable efficacy, preserving them as a nation and conferring upon them a mighty power. We find the Trojans 200 years before the building of the temple having possession of a Palladium which fell from heaven, and only by its loss could their city be destroyed. The Chaldeans wore triangular pieces of metal, sometimes stones, on which were engraven certain characters called talismans, the possession of which they imagined gave them power over the spirits and mortals. The principal was named Bel or Baal. In confirmation we find the Jews saying to Christ, "You cast out devils by the aid of Belzebub." The Hindoos have a word of such tremendous efficacy that the simple utterance of the word by a holy Brahmin would shake the paradise of Swerga to its center, convulse the earth to its foundation, restore the dead to life, destroy the living, transport himself where he pleased, and fill him with the wisdom of the gods. This word is Aun or

On, and belongs to the triad. The word On is Egyptian and was esteemed the most ancient of the gods, for Plato, who derived much information from the Egyptians, writes, "Tell me of the god On, which was and is and never knew beginning." They ascribe the same powers to "On" that the Jews did to Jehovah. But the affinity of certain words between Hindoos, Chaldeans and Egyptians is so close that we may presume they came from the same source. The Jews believed by the power of the name. It cured them of evils, warned them of danger, restored the dead to life, brought fire from heaven, rent buildings asunder, maimed and destroyed their enemies, and filled them with great wisdom; the pronunciation shakes heaven and earth, and inspires the very angels with astonishment. The Rabbins call it "Shem Hamphorosh," the unutterable name. That the word inspired the possessor with great wisdom, the sacred records testify in many instances. The first place where we find it in its proper name is in Samuel, who was inspired with so great wisdom as to be judge of the Jews. We find, also, the word had the same power when communicated. Samuel gave the word to Saul, and the possession filled him with wisdom and understanding far above his compeers, and, in the allegorical language of the East, gave him another heart, and so surprised those who knew him as to make them exclaim, "Is this Saul the son of Kish?" But we find on the loss of the word he was greatly troubled and endeavored to regain it in various ways; at last summoned the spirit of Samuel to give it. Samuel gave the word to David, and the Lord was with David from that day forward, for he says expressly, "For thy word's sake has thy servant known these great things." And we find David triumphing over all his enemies by the power vested in him.

When God refused David to build a temple to his name, Solomon was appointed in his stead, and tradition states, that on commencing the foundation he struck on a cavern in which were immense treasures of gold, silver and precious stones. Believing it to be the remains of some temple built before the flood, and fearing that it had been in the service of idolatry, he was informed by a dream that this place had been thrice devoted to God. It was the place whence Enoch was translated, where Abraham was about to offer up his son Isaac, and it was the place of the threshing-floor of Ornan the Jebusite, where David met and appeased the destroying angel. The treasures were collected and used in building the temple. On exploring the lowest recesses of the cavern they came upon an arched vault, in which they found a white marble pillar, on which, encrusted with precious stones, was a delta, and on which was engraved the Gr∴ Om∴ word, the possession of which filled him with such wisdom and understanding that his name resounded throughout the earth, and has so continued to the present day. It was this that enabled our three Grand Masters to erect such a magnificent structure, the like of which has not been before or since.

The Arabians have the tradition that the word was engraved on a seal, and gave them power over the Dives, Afreets, Ghouls and other evil spirits, imprisoning them and confining them at the bottom of the sea, by impressing on them the signet. By them it was called a talisman or conferrer of power. By the Egyptians they were worn as amulets or averters of danger, and are still worn at the present day. We now see by the inspiration it gave its possessor what struck Solomon with such consternation and anxiety on the death of H∴ A∴. The key was probably a triangular plate on which was engraved the Omnific name, this being worn constantly on the breast, would, by lying on it continually, give a faint impression of the word; * * *. It was the possession of the word * * *. Having mentioned that all nations possessed a word, we will inquire how it first came in possession of the Jews. The Rabbinical tradition is, that it was given by God to Adam, who, foreseeing the deluge, enjoined on the sons of Seth to preserve it for future generations, when the flood would have swept all but Noah's family away. Enoch the son of Seth, while deliberating upon the best means of preserving for future generations the ineffable name of Deity, was favored by a mystical vision, he seemed to be transported to the top of a high mountain. On looking up, he discovered in the heavens a triangular plate brilliantly illuminated, on which appeared certain mystic characters which he received a strict injunction never to pronounce; he then appeared to descend to the bowels of the earth; looking beneath him he discovered the same triangle. Instructed by this vision he built two pillars, on which was engraven the knowledge of the antediluvian world, and beneath he formed a cavern, and in it he deposited the triangle on which was engraved the ineffable word. He left a key to the name, as our Grand Masters have done, so those who had this key could pronounce the name. The Eastern nations have the tradition that the key left was composed of small squares joined together, called a Zuarga, which they consult at the present day, as to matters of health and business. It is possible that the key to the R∴ A∴ W∴ is the Zuarga of the East.

The ineffable name was pronounced once a year by the High-Priest, amid the clang of cymbols and sound of trumpets, at the Feast of Expiation. It was not lawful to pronounce it any other time.

* * * * * *

After the loss of the word, the Jews endeavored to find a substitute by an idol, called by the Rabbins a Teraphim. According to tradition it was constructed in this wise, and occasioned the Jews much trouble in after periods. A head of a child first born and dead born was placed on a golden plate on whose rim was engraved mystic characters. Under the tongue they placed a laminar of gold, on which was engraved characters and inscriptions of certain planets. After performing invocations before it, it was endowed with speech to foretell events. This is the idol that is so bitterly inveighed against by Isaiah, Jeremiah and Ezekiel. This is following after the abomination of the heathen instead of seeking the word.

The Babylonians practised divinations and sorcery, and the Jews copied largely from them, and were in full force from their return from Babylon till the destruction of the temple by Titus, and thus has been transmitted down to us the various rites, mystic ceremonies and charms yet practised among the ignorant and uneducated of the present day.

Thus, Companion, have I endeavored to give a brief epitome and slight explanation of such parts of our work as may stimulate your zeal and energies to further enquiries in penetrating the darkness and bringing to light the long lost word in all its effulgent splendor.

CHARGE TO THE CANDIDATE.

COMPANION: Having attained to this degree, you have passed the *circle of perfection* in ancient Masonry. In the capacity of Select Master you must be sensible that your obligations are increased in proportion to your privileges. Let it be your constant care to prove yourself worthy of the confidence reposed in you, and of the high honor conferred, in admitting you to this select degree. Let uprightness and integrity attend your steps; let *justice* and *mercy* mark your conduct; let *fervency* and *zeal* stimulate you in the discharge of the various duties incumbent upon you; but suffer not an idle or impertinent *curiosity* to lead you astray, or betray you into danger. Be *deaf* to every insinuation which would have a tendency to weaken your resolution, or tempt you to an act of *disobedience*. Be voluntarily *dumb* and *blind*, when the exercise of those faculties would endanger the peace of your mind, or the probity of your conduct; and let *silence* and *secrecy*, those cardinal virtues of a Select Master, on all necessary occasions, be scrupulously observed. By a steady adherence to the important instructions contained in this degree, you will merit the approbation of the select number with whom you are associated, and will enjoy the high satisfaction of having acted well your part in the important enterprise in which you are engaged, and, after having *wrought your regular hours*, may be admitted to participate in all the privileges of a *Select Master*.

CHARGE AT CLOSING.

COMPANIONS : Being about to quit this sacred retreat, to mix again with the world, let us not forget, amid the cares and vicissitudes of active life, the bright example of sincere friendship, so beautifully illustrated in the lives of the founders of this degree. Let us take the lesson home with us; and may it strengthen the bands of fraternal love between us; incite our hearts to duty, and our desires to wisdom. Let us exercise Charity, cherish Hope, walk in Faith. And may that moral principle, which is the mystic cement of our fellowship, remain with and bless us. So mote it be.

SUPER-EXCELLENT MASTER.

HIS degree has no connection, either in symbolism or history, with the degrees of Royal and Select Master. It refers to circumstances which occurred during the siege of Jerusalem by Nebuzaradan, Captain of the Guard of the King of Babylon. The ceremonies are intended to represent the final destruction of the Temple and the carrying away of the captive Jews to Babylon, and exemplifies a part of the Royal Arch degree.

The degree, no doubt, comes from the Ancient and Accepted Rite, and was originally conferred by the Inspectors General of that rite. It is now conferred in many of the jurisdictions in Councils of Royal and Select Masters. The moral of the degree is intended to inculcate integrity and fidelity to vows; and the treachery of Zedekiah is illustrated as a warning to remain faithful to our engagements.

The officers of a Council of Super-Excellent Masters are as follows:

38   CRYPTIC MASONRY.

1. ZEDEKIAH, King of Judah, styled M∴ Ex∴ K∴
2. COMPANION GEDELIAH;
3. FIRST KEEPER OF THE TEMPLE;
4. SECOND KEEPER OF THE TEMPLE:
5. THIRD KEEPER OF THE TEMPLE;
6. CAPTAIN OF THE GUARDS;
7. FIRST HERALD;
8. SECOND HERALD;
9. THIRD HERALD:
10. GUARD,
11. GUARD, } Attendants to the K∴
12. GUARD,
13. TREASURER;
14. SECRETARY;
15. SENTINEL.

The officers are stationed as follows:

Guards attend King (10, 11, 12.)

RECEPTION:

* * * * * *

* * * * * *

* * * * * *

* * * * * *

* * * * * *

SUPER-EXCELLENT MASTER. 41

* * * * * *

The King and all his men-of-war fled by night by the way of the gate between the walls which is by the King's garden, and the King went the way toward the plain, and the army of the Chaldeans pursued after the King and overtook him on the plains of Jericho—and all his army was scattered from him. So they took the King and brought him up to the King of Babylon, to Riblah, and they gave judgment upon him; and they slew the sons of Zedekiah before his eyes, and they put out the eyes of Zedekiah and bound him in chains of brass and carried him to Babylon.

The sword of the enemy prevails, our young men are captives and our old men are slain.

* * * * * *

* * * * * *

How doth the city sit solitary that was full of people; how is she become as a widow! she that was great among the nations and princess among the provinces, how is she become tributary! She weepeth sore in the night, and her tears are on her cheeks: among all her lovers she hath none to comfort her: all her friends have dealt treacherously with her, they are become her enemies.—LAMENTATIONS, i. 1–2.

SUPER-EXCELLET MASTER. 45

HYMN:

Air—*St Martin, or Balerma.*

By Babel's stream we sit and weep,
  Our tears for Zion flow;
Our harps on drooping willows sleep,
  Our hearts are filled with woe.

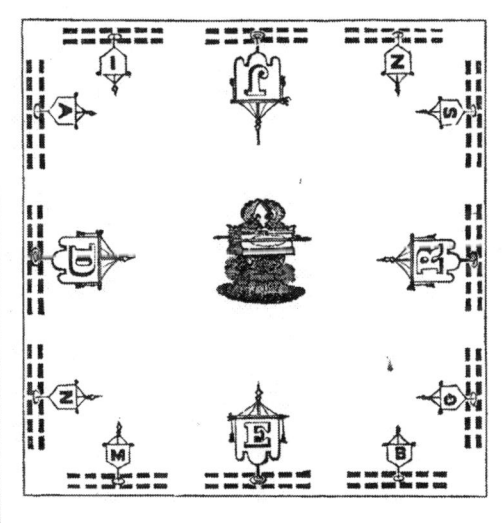

* * * * * *

"And on the east side toward the rising sun shall they of the standard of the camp of Judah, pitch with Isaacher and Zebulon."

"On the south side the standard of the camp of Reuben, with Simeon and Gad."

"On the west side the standard of the camp of Ephraim, with Manasseh and Benjamin."

"On the north side the standard of the camp of Dan, with Asher and Napthali."

"Then the Tabernacle of the congregation shall set forward with the camp of the Levites in the midst of the camp."

By the rivers of Babylon, there we sat down, yea, we wept, when we remembered Zion. We hanged our harps on the willows in the midst thereof. For there they that carried us away captive required of us a song; and they that wasteth us required of us mirth, saying, Sing us one of the songs of Zion.—PSALM cxxxvii. 1-3.

Our walls no more resound with praise,
    Our Temple, foes destroy;
Judea's courts no more upraise
    Triumphant songs of joy.

*   *   *   *   *   *

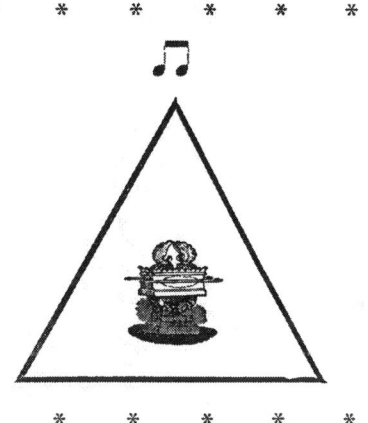

*   *   *   *   *   *

Judah is gone into captivity because of affliction, and because of great servitude; she dwelleth among the heathen, she findeth no rest; all her persecutors overtook her between the straits. The ways of Zion do mourn, because none come to the solemn feasts; all her gates are desolate; her priests sigh, her virgins are afflicted, and she is in bitterness.—LAMENTATIONS, i., 3–4.

How shall we sing the Lord's song in a strange land? If I forget thee, O Jerusalem, let my right hand forget her cunning.—PSALM cxxxvii. 4–5.

Here, mourning, toil the captive bands,
    Our feasts and Sabbaths cease;
Our tribes, dispersed through distant lands,
    Are hopeless of release.

* * * * * *

* * * * * *

The word of Jeremiah the prophet, to the captives in Babylon, saying, This captivity is long. Build ye houses and dwell in them: and plant gardens, and eat the fruit of them; And seek the peace of the city whither I have caused you to be carried away captives, and pray unto the Lord for it; for in the peace thereof shall ye have peace.—Jer. xxix. 5, 7.

If I do not remember thee, let my tongue cleave to the roof of my mouth; if I prefer not Jerusalem above my chief joy.—Psalm cxxxvii. 6.

* * * * * *

But should the ever gracious Power
    To us propitious be,
Chaldeans shall our race restore,
    And kings proclaim us free.

♩

* * * * * *

HISTORY.

The ceremonies through which you have passed have a moral and historic significance.

The *historic* alludes to the taking of Jerusalem, and the destruction of the Temple by Nebuchadnezzar, King of Babylon.

Zedekiah who reigned at this time in Jerusalem was the uncle of Jehoiachim, the youthful king placed at eighteen years of age upon the throne.

The former name of Zedekiah was Mattaniah. The change of name was to indicate that the *justice*, and not the *gift* of the Lord, imparted to him a scepter at the pleasure of the Babylonish monarch.

Nebuchadnezzar's final and fatal siege of Jerusalem began on Friday the 30th of December, in the 588th year before the Christian Era, being the seventh year of Pharaoh Hophra, King of Egypt.

The King of Judah besought the aid of Egypt against the Chaldeans. Pharaoh attempted to interpose, but the result was to no purpose, as the prophet had foretold.

Pharaoh's demonstration only occasioned an intermission of the siege for a period of about one hundred days. The city yielded to the Chaldean power and to famine on Wednesday, the thirteenth of June.

Deducting from the 530 days since the forts were built about Jerusalem, the probable interval of 100 days, wherein Pharaoh diverted the attention of the Chaldeans, and we have the 430 days during which Ezekiel was called upon prophetically to bear the iniquities of Israel and Judah.

Zedekiah, dreading the fury of the monarch to whom he owed his own elevation, had fled from the city, but was pursued by the Chaldeans and captured in the plains of Jericho, about eighteen miles from Jerusalem.

Northward from this, 100 miles distant, was Riblah, in the region of Hamath, where Pharaoh Nechi had put in bonds the humiliated Jehoahas, son of Josiah.

At this place Nebuchadnezzar now had his quarters, and to him the troops conducted the captive Zedekiah: "And they slew the sons of Zedekiah before his eyes, and put out the eyes of Zedekiah and bound him with fetters of brass and carried him to Babylon." Thus were verified what had seemed to be the contradictory prophecies of Jeremiah and Ezekiel. The former predicting of Zedekiah: "Thine eyes shall behold the eyes of the king of Babylon, and he shall speak with thee mouth to mouth, and thou shalt go to Babylon." And the latter announcing, "I will bring him to Babylon to the land of the Chaldeans, yet he shall not see it though he shall die there."

Nebuzaradan, the commanding officer of the Chaldean army presented himself at Jerusalem on Wednesday, the 11th of the succeeding month, and on the following Sabbath, the 14th of July, he completed his cruel and profane ravage in plundering and burning the Temple and city.

The history prepares us for the thrilling and sacred theme of the pious and wonderful rebuilding of the Lord's house. The *moral* purpose of this degree is to inculcate true devotion in spirit and in truth to the Great I AM, in contradistinction to idolatry; to teach traditionally life's vicissitudes; to encourage generous hospitality and friendship; to enlighten the mind and amend the heart, that we may become wiser and purer, brighter and brighter unto the perfect day, and by precept and example to excite our Brethren to moral action and the amiable practice of sincere devotion toward God, and of all the social virtues. It also inculcates the faithful fulfillment of our several vows, and the fearless discharge of our respective duties; and teaches us, that the violation of our solemn vows, as in the case of Zedekiah, the last king of Judah, will not only cause us to forfeit the respect and friendship of our Companions, but will also most surely destroy our own peace of mind.

Then let us, my Companions, labor diligently and fearlessly in the cause of Truth our allotted time, doing with our might whatever our hands find to do, so that, when at the time of the third watch our work is finished, we may be greeted as Super-Excellent Masters, and be released from our captivity in the flesh, to return over the rough and rugged way of the valley of the Shadow of Death to our abiding-place, eternal in the heavens, there to erect our last and perfect moral and Masonic Temple and adore the Holy One of Israel throughout the endless cycles of eternity.

INSTALLATION OF THE OFFICERS

OF A

SUBORDINATE COUNCIL.

FFICERS of Subordinate Councils may be installed by any present or Past Grand Officer, or by any present or Past Master of a Council in good standing in any regularly constituted Council of Royal and Select Masters.

The Council being duly assembled and in working order, the installing officer shall direct the Recorder to read so much of the records as refer to the election of the officers presenting themselves for installation.

After which he shall say:

Companions of ―― Council, No.―, do you remain satisfied with the choice you have made in the selection of your officers for the ensuing Masonic year?

The answer being in the affirmative, the officers elect shall be arranged by the Marshal (an officer to be appointed for the occasion) in due form in front of the installing officer, when they shall be required to make the following

DECLARATION:

I, ——, do solemnly promise that I will faithfully, and to the best of my ability discharge the duties of the office to which I have been elected in this Council, and that I will strictly conform to the requirements of the By-Laws of this Council, and the Constitutions and General Regulations of the Most Puissant Grand Council of the State of —— —— so far as they may come to my knowledge.

The officers elect shall then resume their seats among the Companions.

The following, or some suitable prayer, shall then be delivered by the Chaplain:

PRAYER.

Most Holy and Glorious Lord God, the Great and Mighty Father of all men, we, Thy humble servants, desire to approach Thee with all reverence, and to implore Thy blessing upon the Companions selected to preside over and conduct the affairs of this Council, and now before Thee. Fill their hearts, we beseech Thee, with Thy fear, that their tongues and actions may promote Thy glory. Make them steadfast in Thy service. Grant them firmness of mind. Animate their hearts and strengthen their endeavors. May they be enabled to teach Thy judgments and Thy laws. Bless them, O Lord, and bless the work of their hands. Accept us in mercy. Hear Thou from Heaven, Thy dwelling-place, and forgive our transgressions. Glory be to God as it was in the beginning, is now, and ever shall be, world without end. Amen.

RESPONSE: So mote it be.

The Marshal will then present the officers elect severally, according to rank, for installation.

Addressing the installing officer, by his proper Masonic title, he shall say:

——, I present to you Companion ——, for installation as —— of this Council. I find him to be well skilled in the Royal Mysteries, zealous in diffusing the sacred principles of our fathers, and in whose integrity and fidelity his Companions of ——

Council, No. —, repose the highest confidence.

The installing officer will then complete the ceremonies by delivering the following Address and Charges, severally, to the officers elect, as they are severally presented to him, according to rank, by the Marshal:

ADDRESS AND CHARGE TO THE MASTER.

THRICE ILLUSTRIOUS COMPANION: I feel great pleasure in receiving you as the presiding officer of this Council. It is a station highly honorable to him who diligently and faithfully performs the duties it imposes upon him. Before investing you, however, with the appropriate insignia of your office, I must require your unequivocal assent to the following interrogatories:

1. Do you solemnly promise that you will use your best endeavors to correct the vices and purify the morals of your Companions, and to promote the peace and prosperity of your Council?

2. That you will not suffer your Council to be opened when there are less than nine

or more than twenty-seven Select Masters present?

3. That you will not suffer any one to pass the circle of perfection in your Council, in whose integrity, fervency and zeal you have not entire confidence?

4. That you will not acknowledge or hold intercourse with any Council that does not work under some regular and constitutional authority?

5. That you will not admit a visitor into your Council who has not been regularly and lawfully invested with the degrees conferred therein, without his having previously been formally healed?

6. That you will faithfully observe and support such By-Laws as may be made by your Council, in conformity with the Constitutions and General Regulations of the Order?

7. That you will pay due respect and obedience to the Grand Officers, when duly installed, and sustain them in the discharge of their lawful duties?

8. Do you submit to these requirements, and promise to observe and practice them faithfully?

RESPONSE: I do.

With entire confidence in the rectitude of your intentions, and in the integrity of your character as a Select Master, I now invest you with the appropriate insignia of your office.

Having been honored with the free suffrages of your Companions, and elevated to the highest office within their gift, it becomes your duty to set them an example of diligence, industry and fidelity; to see that the officers associated with you faithfully perform their respective duties, and that the interest and reputation of your Council are not endangered by imprudence or neglect. The important trusts committed to your charge will call forth your best exertions, and the exercise of your best faculties.

As the representative of the wise King of Israel, it will be your duty to recite the secret traditions, and illustrate the moral principles of the Order, to cherish the worthy, and to hold in due veneration the ancient landmarks.

By a frequent recurrence to the By-laws of your Council, and the General Regulations and Constitutions of the Grand Council, you will be enabled to fulfill the important obligations resting upon you with honor to yourself and with credit to the Craft.

And may He, without whose approving smiles our labors are all in vain, give strength to your endeavors and support to your exertions.

CHARGE TO THE DEPUTY MASTER.

RT. ILLUSTRIOUS COMPANION : Having been elected to the second office in this Council, I, with great pleasure, invest you with the insignia of your office.

The duties of the important office to which your Companions have elevated you will require your constant and earnest attention. You are to occupy the second seat in the

Council, and it will be your duty to aid and support your chief in all the requirements of his office. In his absence you will be called upon to preside in the Council, and to discharge all the important duties annexed to his station.

Although the representative of a king, and elevated in rank above your Companions, yet may you never forget that in all the duties you owe to God, your neighbor and yourself, you and they stand upon the same level of equality. Let the bright example of your predecessor in the Grand Council at Jerusalem stimulate you to the faithful performance of every duty, and when the King of kings shall summon you to His immediate presence, may you receive from His hand a crown of glory that shall never fade away.

CHARGE TO THE PRINCIPAL CONDUCTOR OF THE WORK.

ILLUSTRIOUS COMPANION: As the third officer of this Council, I now invest you with the insignia of your office. It is your duty to sound the silver trumpet at early dawn and eve of day, when the sun's first and last beams gild the mountain-tops, to announce high noon, and proclaim the time of rest and labor.

In the absence of either of your superior officers, you will be required to perform the duties annexed to his station respectively; and as the interests of your Council ought never to suffer from the want of intelligence in its officers, you will allow me to urge upon you the necessity of being always qualified and fully prepared to meet the emergency, should it ever arise.

Having been admitted to the *fellowship of Kings*, you will be frequently reminded that the office of *mediator* is both honorable and praiseworthy. Let it therefore be your constant care to preserve harmony and unanimity of sentiment among the members of your Council. Discountenance whatever may tend to create divisions and dissensions among the Brethren in any of the departments of Masonry. And as the glorious sun at its meridian dispels the mists and clouds that obscure the horizon, so may your exertions tend to dissipate the mist of jealousy and discord, should any such ever unfortunately arise in your Council.

CHARGE TO THE RECORDER.

COMPANION: I now invest you with the insignia of your office. The qualities which should distinguish you in discharging the various duties annexed to your station are, correctness in recording the proceedings of your Council; judgment in discriminating between what is proper and what is improper to be written; regularity in making the returns to the Grand Council; integrity in accounting for all moneys that may pass through your hands, and fidelity in paying the same over to the Treasurer. The possession of these qualities has designated you as a suitable Companion for the important office to which you have been elected, and I entertain no doubt but that you will discharge all the duties incumbent on you with fidelity and honor. And when you shall have completed the records of your transactions here below, and finished the term of your probation, may you be admitted to the Grand Council above, and find your name recorded in the book of life.

CHARGE TO THE TREASURER.

COMPANION: You have been elected to a very important and responsible office in this Council, and I now, with pleasure invest you with the insignia of your office. It is your duty to number and weigh out the shekels of the sanctuary, and to provide for the helpless orphan. The qualities which should distinguish you are accuracy and fidelity; accuracy in keeping a fair and true account of the receipts and disbursements; fidelity in carefully preserving the property and funds of the Council, and in rendering a just account of the same when required.

Your interest in this Council, your attachment to the Craft, and your known integrity of character, are a sure guaranty that your duties will be faithfully performed.

CHARGE TO THE CAPTAIN OF THE GUARD.

Companion: Having been appointed Captain of the Guard in this Council, I present you with the insignia of your office. Guard well your post, and suffer none to pass it but the *select*, the faithful and the worthy. Be ever attentive to the commands of your chief, and be always near at hand to see them duly executed.

CHARGE TO THE CONDUCTOR.

Companion: The office to which you have been appointed is one of much importance in the proceedings of this Council. In the discharge of the duties appertaining to it, and with which you are doubtless familiar, be fervent and zealous; you will thus secure the respect and esteem of your Companions, and the approbation of your own conscience.

You will now assume your station.

CHARGE TO THE CHAPLAIN.

Rev. Companion: You have been appointed Chaplain of this Council. Your good inclinations will undoubtedly aid you in the performance of those solemn services which created beings should constantly render to their Great Creator, and which, when offered by one whose holy profession it is *to point to Heaven and lead the way*, may, by refining our morals, strengthening our virtues, and purifying our minds, prepare us for admission into the presence of our Supreme Grand Master, where happiness will be as perfect as it is endless.

CHARGE TO THE MARSHAL.

Companion: The duties of your office require but little elucidation. It is your duty, in connection with the Conductor, to attend to the examination of visitors, and to take special care that none are permitted to enter but such as have proved their title to our favor and friendship. I present you with the implement of your office, in the confident belief that it is intrusted to competent and faithful hands.

CHARGE TO THE STEWARD AND SENTINEL.

COMPANIONS: You have been appointed to the office of Steward and Sentinel, respectively, and I now, with pleasure, invest you with the appropriate insignia of your office. Let the sword placed in your hands serve as a constant admonition to you to set a guard at the entrance of your thoughts, to place a watch at the door of your lips, to post a sentinel at the avenues of your affections, thereby excluding every unworthy thought, word and deed, and enabling you to preserve your consciences void of offense toward God and man.

CHARGE TO THE COUNCIL.

WORTHY AND BELOVED COMPANIONS: From the nature of our beloved institution, some must of necessity *rule* and others *obey*. And while justice and moderation are required of the officers in the discharge of their official duties, subordination and respect for their rulers are equally demanded of the members. *The relation is reciprocal.* The interests of both are inseparable, and without mutual coöperation the labors of neither can succeed. Let the avenues to your passions be strictly guarded. Let no curious intruder find his way into the secret recesses of your retirement, to disturb the harmony which should ever prevail among the *select* and *chosen.* In so doing, you will best secure the prosperity of your Council, the respect of your Companions and the commendation of your own consciences.

The Installing Officer shall then make the following declaration:

By virtue of the powers in me vested, I do now declare the officers of .... Council, No. ..., regularly installed, in due and ancient form.

The Chaplain shall then conclude the installation ceremonies by delivering the following, or some suitable form of

PRAYER.

Eternal and ever blessed Jehovah, most humbly do we beseech Thee to look down with an eye of favor upon this Council, now assembled before Thee. Bless, if it shall please Thee, the proceedings of this hour, and grant that every transaction of this body may tend to Thy glory and to our advancement in knowledge and virtue, and to Thy great name shall be ascribed eternal praises, world without end. Amen.

RESPONSE: So mote it be.

ORDER OF CEREMONIES

IN

CONSTITUTING AND DEDICATING COUNCILS

OF

ROYAL AND SELECT MASTERS.

HE new Council shall assemble in their hall and be called to order by their presiding officer.

The Grand Council will meet and open in an adjoining room.

A Committee from the new Council shall inform the Grand Marshal that the new Council is prepared to receive the Grand Council. The Grand Marshal will announce the same to the Grand Master.

The Committee shall then conduct the Grand Council to the Hall of the new Council, where they shall be received with the usual honors.

The officers of the new Council shall then resign their seats to the Grand officers, and cause their jewels to be laid upon the altar and covered.

An Ode shall then be sung, or an appropriate piece of music be performed, after which the Grand Chaplain shall repeat the following, or some other suitable form of

PRAYER.

Almighty and Supreme Architect of the Universe, Maker and Ruler of all things, who is there in Heaven but Thee, and who upon earth can stand in competition with Thee? Thine omniscient mind brings all things in review, past, present, and to come. Thine omnipotent arm directs the movements of the vast creation. Thine omnipresent eye pervades the secret recesses of every heart. Thy boundless beneficence supplies us with every comfort and enjoyment. Thy unspeakable perfections and glory surpass the understanding of the children of men. We do most humbly invoke Thy special blessings upon the purposes of our present assembly. Let this Council be established to thy honor and glory. May its officers be endowed with wisdom to discern and fidelity to pursue its true interests. May its members be ever mindful of the duty they owe to their God, the obedience they owe to their superiors,

CONSTITUTING AND DEDICATING. 73

the love they owe to their equals, and the good-will they owe to all mankind. May this Council be erected to Thy glory, and may its members ever exemplify their love to thee by their beneficence to their fellow-man, and eventually enjoy the rewards of a well-spent life in the sacred sanctuary on high. Glory be to God, as it was in the beginning, is now, and ever shall be, world without end. Amen.

RESPONSE: So mote it be.

Should time permit, an oration or some suitable address may now be delivered.

The Grand Marshal shall then address the Grand Master in the words following, viz:

MOST PUISSANT GRAND MASTER: A constitutional number of Companions, duly instructed in the sublime mysteries, having received from the Grand Council a Charter, authorizing them to open and hold a regular Council of Royal and Select Masters in this place, are now assembled for the purpose of having the same legally constituted and solemnly dedicated in *ample* form.

The Charter granted the new Council shall then be read by the Grand Recorder.

The Grand Master will then address the Companions forming the new Council as follows:

COMPANIONS: Do you accept the Charter which has just been read in your hearing by the Grand Recorder, and do you promise to perform all the requirements therein contained, conforming in all your Masonic workings to the Constitutions, By-Laws and General Regulations of the Most Puissant Grand Council of the State of ——— ———?

The answer being in the affirmative, the Grand Master shall proceed as follows:

By virtue of the high power in me vested as Grand Master of Royal and Select Masters of the State of ——— ———, I do now form and constitute you, my worthy Companions, into a regular Council of Royal and Select Masters, by the name of ...... Council, No. ....; and I hereby authorize and empower you and your successors to open and hold said Council, and to do and perform all such things as may appertain thereunto, conforming in all things to the Constitutions, By-Laws, and General Regulations of the Most Puissant Grand Council of the State of ———— ————. And may the God of our fathers be with you to guide and direct you in all your doings. Amen.

RESPONSE: So mote it be.

An Ode or Hymn shall then be sung, or a suitable piece of music performed, during which the Grand Marshal shall uncover the jewels.

The following Dedicatory Declaration shall then be pronounced by the Grand Master:

To our Ancient and Most Puissant Grand Master Solomon, King of Israel, we solemnly dedicate this Council. May the blessings of him who presides in the Grand Council above rest upon all the members thereof, and may He so direct their labors that His name may be magnified, now and ever. Amen.

RESPONSE: So mote it be.

The following proclamation shall then be made by the Grand Marshal:

I am directed by the Most Puissant Grand Master to proclaim, and I do hereby proclaim this Council, by the name of ...... Council, No. ...., duly constituted and dedicated, this ...... day of ......, A. D.....

Should it be deemed desirable, another suitable piece of music may be now performed, when the ceremonies shall close with the following benediction, to be pronounced by the Grand Chaplain:

BENEDICTION.

May the blessing of the God of Abraham, the God of Isaac, and the God of Jacob rest upon and be with you always, now and forever. Amen.

RESPONSE: So mote it be.

Should any other officer than the Grand Master officiate at the dedicatory ceremonies, the word *ample* is to be omitted wherever it occurs in the service, and in place thereof shall be used the words "*in due and ancient form.*"

INSTALLATION OF THE OFFICERS

OF THE

GRAND COUNCIL.

AT the time appointed for the Installation, the Grand Council being regularly opened, the Chair must be taken by some Grand or Past Grand Master; or, if none be present, by the highest Grand or Past Grand Officer, who is, or has been, a presiding officer in a Subordinate Council.

The R. P. Grand Marshal shall then introduce the Grand Master elect to the Installing Officer, saying:

MOST PUISSANT: I present to you Companion ......, who, having been duly elected Grand Master of the Grand Council of the State of ———— ————, for the ensuing Masonic year, now declares himself ready for installation.

The Installing Officer shall then address the members of the Grand Council, saying:

COMPANIONS OF THE GRAND COUNCIL: Companion ......, having been duly elected to preside over you as your Grand Master, now declares himself ready for installation. If any of you can show just cause why he should not be installed, you will make your objections now known, or forever after hold your peace.

If objections are made, the Grand Council shall proceed at once to hear and determine the same.

If no objections are made, he shall continue to say,

No cause being shown to the contrary, I shall now proceed to install him.

The Installing Officer shall then administer the following Obligation of Office, all the companions standing:

I, ..., do solemnly promise and swear that I will serve as Grand Master of the Grand Council of the State of ......, for the term for which I have been elected, and will, to the best of my abilities, faithfully discharge the duties appertaining to that office. I do furthermore promise and swear that I will support and maintain the Constitutions of this Grand Council, and inviolably preserve the ancient landmarks of the Order. So help me God.

The Grand Chaplain shall then offer the following prayer:

O thou most holy and omnipotent Lord God of heaven and earth! we do most humbly beseech thee to smile upon and bless this Grand Council now assembled. Sanctify unto each one of us now present the transactions of this hour. Make us humble and thankful recipients of all the bounties Thou art continually bestowing upon us, and move our hearts with impulses of tenderness and charity toward all men, and especially toward those who have wrought with us their regular hours in the secret vault. Bestow upon us, we beseech Thee, a portion of Thine infinite Wisdom, and especially upon him who has been selected to preside over this Grand Council. Take from him all pride of heart, stubbornness of will, and self-sufficiency of understanding, and all vanity, ostentation and arrogance, if any such he have; and give him in their stead a meekness and lowliness of heart, and a kindness and gentleness of disposition, that shall cause him to rule and govern his Companions with love and affection, and in thy fear.

And we pray Thee, O Lord God, that, when our labors here are ended, and the hour of everlasting rest has arrived, we may be received into the Grand Council above, and hear the thrilling welcome, "Come, ye blessed of my Father, into the mansions prepared for you from the beginning of the world." Amen.

RESPONSE BY THE COMPANIONS: So mote it be.

The Installing Officer then invests the Grand Master elect with the insignia of his office, and proceeds with the following

CHARGE.

By the voice of your Companions, you have been elevated to the highest office within their gift; and as they rely with entire confidence upon the rectitude of your intentions and the integrity of your character, it becomes your duty to set them an example of diligence, industry and fidelity; to see that the officers associated with you faithfully perform their respective duties; and that the reputation and interests of this Grand Council are not endangered by imprudence or neglect.

The important trust committed to your charge will call for your best exertions, and the exercise of your best faculties. As the representative of the wise King of Israel, it will be your duty to recite the secret traditions, to illustrate the moral principles of the Order, to cherish the worthy, and to hold in due veneration the ancient landmarks of our time-honored institution.

The purple robe, the crown and the scepter are emblems of union and authority. They are to indicate to you that, while you govern your Companions with mildness, firmness and impartiality, you are to teach them lessons of union and harmony, which are the chief supports in our great Masonic edifice. And as you are seated in the East, the place of light and heat, so you are to be the source of light and heat to those under your charge. Enlighten them with a knowledge of our traditions, our forms and ceremonies; the signification of our tools and emblems, and the general arts and mysteries of our Craft; and impart to them a portion of the warmth of zeal and devotion that burns in your own bosom.

By a frequent recurrence to the Constitutions of this Grand Council, and the general regulations of the Fraternity, together with a constant observance of the great principles inculcated in the various lectures and charges, you will be enabled to fulfill the important obligations resting upon you with honor to yourself and credit to the Craft. And may He, without whose approving smiles our labors are all in vain, give strength to your endeavors and support to your exertions.

The Grand Master elect shall then take his seat in the East, and assume the gavel. After which (all the Companions standing) the Grand Captain of the Guard shall make proclamation thus:

COMPANIONS: In the name of the Most High God, I do proclaim Most Puissant

Companion, ..., Grand Master of the Grand Council of the State of ......, for the term prescribed by the Constitutions.

The remaining Officers elect, standing in order before the officiating Officer, shall then make the following declaration:

I, ..., do solemnly promise that I will faithfully, and to the best of my ability, discharge the duties of the office to which I have been elected, and that I will strictly conform to the requirements of the Constitutions of the Grand Council of the State of ...., together with the General Regulations of the Order, so far as they may come to my knowledge.

After which the officers elect shall kneel (the rest of the Companions present standing), while the R. P. Grand Chaplain repeats the following.

PRAYER.

Most Holy and Glorious Lord God, the Great Architect of Heaven and Earth, we approach Thee with reverence, and implore Thy blessing on these Companions, selected to assist our presiding officer in conducting the business of this Grand Council, and now prostrate before Thee. Fill their hearts with Thy fear, that their tongues and actions may promote Thy glory. Make them steadfast in Thy service. Grant them wisdom, that they may teach Thy judgments and Thy laws. Animate their hearts and strengthen their endeavors. Bless them, O Lord, and bless the work of their hands. Accept us in mercy. Hear Thou, from Heaven, Thy dwelling-place, and forgive our transgressions. Amen.

Response: So mote it be.

The R. P. Grand Marshal will now present each of the remaining Grand Officers elect in order, according to rank, when they shall be charged by the Installing Officer, respectively, as follows:

(After each charge, the R. P. Grand Marshal shall conduct the officer elect, so charged, to his proper position in the Grand Council Chamber.)

CHARGE TO THE DEPUTY GRAND MASTER.

Right Puissant Companion: Have you attended to the important obligation taken by your superior, and do you promise to support

INSTALLATION CEREMONIES.

all the ancient charges and regulations as freely and fully as he has done?

ANSWER: I do.

The duties of the important office to which your Companions have elected you will require your constant and earnest attention.

You are to occupy the second seat in this Grand Council, and it will be your duty to aid and support your chief in all the requirements of his office. In his absence you will be called upon to preside in the Grand Council, and to discharge all those important duties which now devolve upon him. Let it, therefore, be your unremitting study to acquire such a degree of knowledge and information as will enable you, when called upon, to discharge with promptness and propriety all the important duties annexed to your station.

CHARGE TO THE GRAND ILLUSTRIOUS MASTER.

RIGHT PUISSANT COMPANION: You have been elevated to the third office in the Grand Council. The duties of the important office to which your Companions have elevated you will require your constant and earnest attention. It will be your duty to aid and support your superior officers in all the requirements of their offices. In their absence, you will be called upon to preside in the Grand Council, and to discharge all the important duties annexed to that station. Although the representative of a King, you should never forget that, in all the duties you owe to God, your neighbor, and yourself, you stand upon the same level of equality with the rest of your Companions.

Let the bright example of your illustrious predecessor in the Grand Council at Jerusalem stimulate you to the faithful performance of every duty, and when the King of kings shall summon you to his immediate presence, from His hand may you receive a crown of glory that shall never fade away.

CHARGE TO THE GRAND PRINCIPAL CONDUCTOR OF THE WORK.

RIGHT PUISSANT COMPANION: As the fourth officer of this Grand Council, it will be your duty to sound the silver trumpet at early dawn and eve of day, when the sun's first and last beams gild the mountain-tops, to announce high noon, and proclaim the time of rest and labor.

In the absence of your superiors you will be required to perform their duties; and as the interests of the Grand Council should never be permitted to suffer through want of intelligence in its officers, you will allow me to urge upon you the necessity of being always qualified and prepared to meet the emergency, should any such arise.

Having been admitted to the fellowship of Kings, you will be frequently reminded that the office of *mediator* is both honorable and praiseworthy. Let it, therefore, be your constant care to preserve harmony and unanimity of sentiment among the members of the Grand Council. Discountenance whatever may tend to create division and dissensions among the Companions in any of the departments of Masonry. And as the glorious sun at its meridian dispels the mists and clouds that obscure the horizon, so may your exertions tend to dissipate the mist of jealousy and discord, should any such ever unfortunately arise.

CHARGE TO THE GRAND RECORDER.

RIGHT PUISSANT COMPANION: It is with much pleasure that I install you into the office to which you have been elected by your Companions. The qualities which should recommend a Recorder are: *correctness* in recording the proceedings; *judgment* in discriminating between what is proper and what is improper to be written; *regularity* in attendance upon the Grand Council; *integrity* in accounting for all moneys that may pass through his hands, and *fidelity* in paying the same over to the Grand Treasurer. The possession of these qualities, I have no doubt, has designated you as a suitable Companion for this important office. I have the utmost confidence, therefore, that you will discharge all the duties incumbent on you with fidelity and honor. May God grant that, when you shall have completed the record of your transactions here below, you may be admitted into the Grand Council above, and find your name recorded in the Book of Life.

CHARGE TO THE GRAND TREASURER.

RIGHT PUISSANT COMPANION: You have been elected to an important and responsible station in this Grand Body. It will be your duty to number and weigh out the shekels of the sanctuary, and to provide for the helpless and the destitute. The qualities which should distinguish you are *accuracy* and *fidelity*—accuracy in keeping a true and fair account of the receipts and disbursements; fidelity in carefully preserving the property and funds of the Grand Council, and in rendering a just account of the same when required. Your interest in this Grand

Council, your attachment to the Craft, and your known integrity of character, are a sufficient guarantee that these duties will be faithfully performed.

CHARGE TO THE GRAND CAPTAIN OF THE GUARD.

RIGHT PUISSANT COMPANION: Having been appointed Captain of the Guard of this Grand Council, I present you with the insignia of your office. Guard well your post, and suffer none to pass it but the select, the faithful, and the true. Be ever attentive to the commands of your chief, and be always near at hand to see them duly executed.

CHARGE TO THE GRAND CHAPLAINS.

RIGHT PUISSANT AND REV. COMPANIONS: You have been appointed Chaplains of this Grand Council. Your good inclinations will undoubtedly aid you in the performance of those solemn services which created beings should constantly render to their Great Creator, and which, when offered by one whose holy profession it is *to point to Heaven and lead the way,* may, by refining our morals, strengthening our virtues, and purifying our minds, prepare us for admission into the presence of our Supreme Grand Master, where happiness will be as perfect as it is endless.

CHARGE TO THE GRAND MARSHAL.

RIGHT PUISSANT COMPANION : The office to which you have been appointed is one of much importance in the proceedings of this Grand Council. In the discharge of the duties appertaining to it, and with which you are familiar, be fervent and zealous. Let uprightness and integrity attend your steps; let *justice* and *mercy* mark your conduct, and predominate in all your actions through life. You will now assume your station.

CHARGE TO THE GRAND STEWARD AND SENTINEL.

PUISSANT COMPANIONS: You are appointed respectively to the office of Grand Steward and Sentinel of this Grand Council, and I now invest you with the implements of your office. As the sword is placed in the hands of the Sentinel to enable him to guard the sanctuary and entrance to the secret passage with sleepless vigilance against intruders, so should it morally serve as a constant admonition to us all to set a guard at the entrance of our thoughts, to place a watch at the door of our lips, to post a sentinel at the avenues of our actions, thereby excluding every unworthy thought, word and deed, and enabling us to preserve our consciences void of offense toward God and man. You will now assume your respective stations.

CHARGE TO THE MEMBERS OF THE GRAND COUNCIL.

COMPANIONS: From the nature of the constitution of every society, some must of necessity *rule* and others *obey*. And while justice and moderation are required of the *officers* in the discharge of their official duties, subordination and respect for their rulers are equally demanded of the *members*. The relation is reciprocal; the interests of both are inseparable, and without mutual coöperation the labors of neither can succeed. A house divided against itself cannot stand. Let, therefore, brotherly love prevail among you; let each be emulous of the others in all good works, and *in no other way*. Let the avenues of your passions be strictly guarded; let no curious intruder find his way into the *secret recesses* of your retirement, to disturb the harmony which should ever prevail among the *select* and *chosen*. In so doing you will secure the prosperity of this Grand Council, the respect of your Companions, the commendation of your own consciences, and, finally, the approval of your Supreme Grand Master and a Crown of Life.

The Grand Marshal shall then make the following proclamation:

I am directed by the Most Puissant Grand Master to proclaim, and I do hereby proclaim, the officers of the Most Puissant

Grand Council of Royal and Select Masters of the State of .... duly and regularly installed in ample form.

The Right Puissant Grand Chaplain shall then offer the following or some suitable prayer, which shall conclude the ceremonies of installation of the Grand Officers:

To Thee, O God, we now commend ourselves, and the varied interests committed to our charge. Ever keep and preserve this Grand Council in purity and usefulness, and may its proceedings tend to Thy glory and the benefit of our race. Amen.

RESPONSE: So mote it be.

More Masonic Books from Cornerstone

The Freemasons Key
A Study of Masonic Symbolism
Edited by Michael R. Poll
6 x 9 Softcover 244 pages
ISBN: 1-887560-97-1

Éliphas Lévi and the Kabbalah
by Robert L. Uzzel
6 x 9 Softcover 208 pages
ISBN: 1-887560-76-9

The Teachings of Freemasonry
by H.L. Haywood
Edited by Michael R. Poll
6x9 Softcover 144 pages
ISBN 1-887560-92-0

A.E. Waite: Words From a Masonic Mystic
Edited by Michael R. Poll
Foreword by Joseph Fort Newton
6 x 9 Softcover 168 pages
ISBN: 1-887560-73-4

Freemasons and Rosicrucians - the Enlightened
by Manly P. Hall
Edited by Michael R. Poll
6 x 9 Softcover 152 pages
ISBN: 1-887560-58-0

Masonic Words and Phrases
Edited by Michael R. Poll
6 x 9 Softcover 116 pages
ISBN: 1-887560-11-4

Cornerstone Book Publishers
www.cornerstonepublishers.com

More Masonic Books from Cornerstone

Masonic Enlightenment
The Philosophy, History and Wisdom of Freemasonry
Edited by Michael R. Poll
6 x 9 Softcover 180 pages
ISBN 1-887560-75-0

God's Soldiers: Roman Catholicism and Freemasonry
by Dudley Wright
6 x 9 Softcover 148 pages
ISBN 1-887560-71-8

Masonic Questions and Answers
by Paul M. Bessel
6 x 9 Softcover 144 pages
ISBN 1-887560-59-9

Our Stations and Places - Masonic Officer's Handbook
by Henry G. Meacham
Revised by Michael R. Poll
6 x 9 Softcover 164 pages
ISBN: 1-887560-63-7

Knights & Freemasons: The Birth of Modern Freemasonry
By Albert Pike & Albert Mackey
Edited by Michael R. Poll
Foreword by S. Brent Morris
6 x 9 Softcover 178 pages
ISBN 1-887560-66-1

Robert's Rules of Order: Masonic Edition
Revised by Michael R. Poll
6 x 9 Softcover 212 pages
ISBN 1-887560-07-6

Cornerstone Book Publishers
www.cornerstonepublishers.com

Made in the USA
San Bernardino, CA
03 December 2012